a comic about being trans male

Morgan Boecher

Artwork by Morgan Boecher
Cover Design & Interior Layout by Erika L. Block
Edited by Stephanie Finnegan

Scout Publishing, LLC
P.O. Box 31214
Omaha, NE 68131
scoutpublishingllc.com

PUBLISHER'S CATALOGING-IN-PUBLICATION DATA:

Boecher, Morgan.

What's Normal Anyway? : a comic about being trans male / Morgan Boecher. -- Second edition. -- Omaha, NE : Scout Publishing, LLC, [2015]

pages : illustrations ; cm.

ISBN: 978-0-9895868-4-9 ; 978-0-9895868-5-6 (ebook)

Summary: A comic that focuses on the coming out and transitional process through the story of Mel, who takes the big risk of being himself and transitioning from female to male. This comic adds another voice representing a part of the wide spectrum of human diversity, and is funny about it too.--Publisher.

1. Gender identity--Fiction. 2. Gender identity--Comic books, strips, etc. 3. Transgender people--Fiction. 4. Transgender people--Comic books, strips, etc. 5. Transsexuals--Fiction. 6. Transsexuals--Comic books, strips, etc. 7. Female-to-male transsexuals--Fiction. 8. Female-to-male transsexuals--Comic books, strips, etc. 9. Sex role--Fiction. 10. Sex role--Comic books, strips, etc. 11. Sex differences--Fiction. 12. Sex differences--Comic books, strips, etc. 13. Graphic novels. 14. Comics (Graphic works) I. Title.

HQ77.9 .B64 2015
306.78/8--dc23   1510

Introduction

A couple of the first thoughts I had when coming out as a trans guy were:

1. Can I still have a happy life?
2. Well, I now have a cool story to tell.

Thought two ended up contributing a great deal to thought one, through this comic before you. After futile attempts to journal my way to truth and catharsis, I turned to my roots of writing and illustrating comics, which got to the point faster and with more humor. Thought three became: Comics are going to help me live through this ordeal.

The physical, social, and emotional transition from female to male felt in a way like holding my humanity way up high, smashing it hard on the floor, and then trying to find all of the pieces that scattered away in order to put the picture back together. What if the job-prospects piece shattered to oblivion? What if I couldn't find the piece that made me attractive? What if the pieces of my friends and family were lost forever?

Chronicling a semifictional version of my transition through *What's Normal Anyway?* helped me realize that one's humanity can never be broken. Rather, those moments when you fall apart are when your humanity is most apparent. Mel, the quirky, bighearted main character, always seems to show his humanity. His story reveals the risks of being this way, but also points to the kinds of friendships and relationships that flourish from being genuine.

It took me a while to get that "being genuine" thing. I entered graduate school with the intention of being a full-time "stealth" man without revealing my trans background. On my first night out with soon-to-be classmates, in a very Mel-like fashion, I presented to my drinking companions business cards inscribed with the *WNA* website and the subtitle "a comic about being trans male." Everyone was impressed that not only did I have a comic, but that I had business cards for it. It wasn't until the next day that I realized that I'd already messed up my plan to be stealth. The magic thing, though, was that talking about my work and being trans was just fine in this group.

Over and over, I found that hiding parts of myself took much more energy than being open. Soon, the loving, supportive people in my life reached critical mass and I had the confidence to be me full-time.

It's still a process figuring out when to come out and to whom, since plenty of people don't know how to react to unexpected gender identities or backgrounds. In this sort of instance the comic helps as a buffer. While *WNA* never meant to be a Trans 101 book, it offers those inexperienced in the gender-variant world a peek into one version of this identity saga. After all, a comic can be much more approachable than a person with toes to step on.

By the end of grad school I enjoyed a sense of having arrived in my gender. It felt like being in a new house after the walls had been painted the right colors and the furniture was all put in place. Not that there wouldn't be redecorating, but for the time being everything was settled. What a relief to be at home!

This turning point heralded the comic's completion. I moved back to New York City after finishing *WNA* in Florida and running a successful crowdfunding campaign to print the book. As fulfilling as it was to make comics, freelancing was tough and I needed a job that would get me out and around people. Now, in the bucolic setting of Westchester, I'm working on other cool stories to tell. All told, coming out and transitioning did not threaten my "happy life." I'm gainfully employed as a creative professional, my eyes get nice compliments, and my friends and family are sticking around. I can't say that I'd be better off without that scramble for those scattered pieces of humanity. It was worth doing and worth laughing about too.

—Morgan Boecher

WHAT IF THEY THINK I DON'T BELONG IN THE SUPPORT GROUP?
I HAVEN'T STARTED HORMONES OR HAD ANY SURGERY!
ALL I'VE GOT IS A SWEATY BINDER!
WELCOME, EVERYONE. WE HAVE A NEW PERSON JOINING THE GROUP TODAY.
WOULD YOU LIKE TO INTRODUCE YOURSELF?
UH, YEAH, HI!
I'M MEL AND I, UH, LIVE IN A TINY ROOM WITH A CAT!
MRB
HI, MEL. WOULD YOU LIKE TO MENTION WHY YOU'RE HERE?
OH, SURE! UH, WELL I'M FTM AND I NEED MORE FRIENDS!
WELCOME!

18

26

27

33

WELL, I DON'T REALLY KNOW HOW I FIT IN WITH ALL OF THIS—

—BUT IT'S COMFORTING TO KNOW THAT I DO.

MRB

54

69

84

HELLO, CAKE. YOU CAN COME WITH ME.
AHHHHH
AHHHH!!!
MRB
DANG IT, BEEF! I FORGOT YOU LIVE HERE!
YEAH, SORRY. GUESS I SHOULD HAVE, UH, KNOCKED OR SOMETHING.
HEY, DUDE, YOU KNOW YOU'VE GOT A PRETTY HOT BOD.
BEEF!

94

107

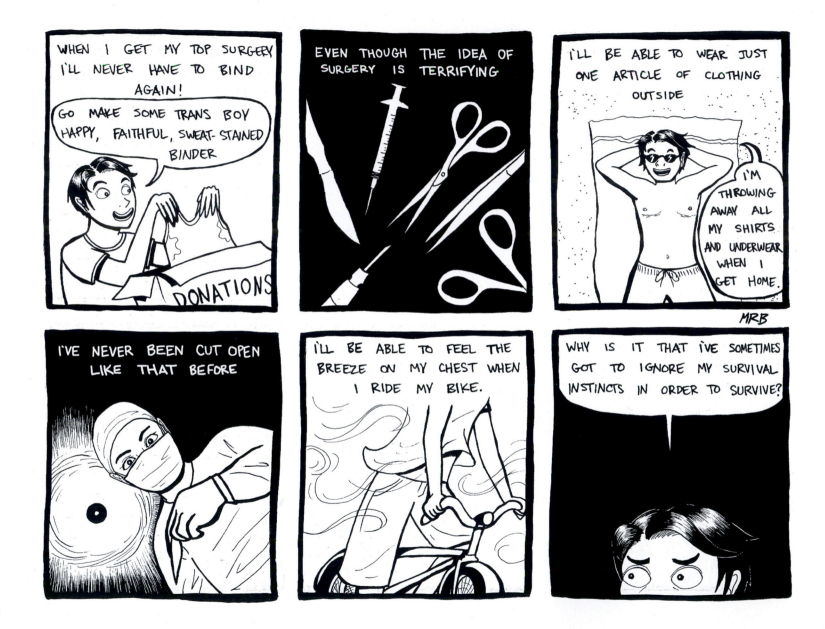

127

129

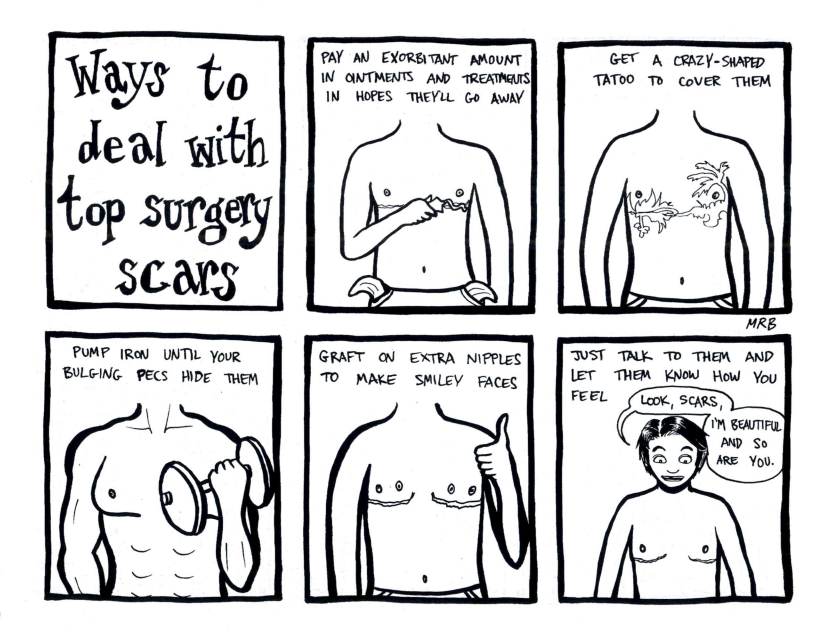

134

141

Acknowledgments

I owe my greatest gratitude to my mom and dad for making their love the surest thing I can count on, and for filling my life with humor from the start. I am grateful for everyone in my family who gifted me their love, trust, and encouragement.

Thanks to all of the Kickstarter supporters who believed in this project and made the first full printing of this comic possible. Thanks to Scout Publishing for carrying this work to the next level.

Thanks to Ian Frazier for bottomless comic inspiration and for talking me through all my worst writer's block.

Thanks to Rio Aubry Taylor for showing me the ropes of the comics world and for being an awesome table mate at comic fests.

I'm grateful for Anna Janosik, who put together WhatsNormalAnyway.net and helpfully responded to my freak-outs when the website was acting up.

I am so deeply grateful for all you readers, friends, supporters, online-comment leavers, and fan-mail senders. Knowing that this comic brightened your day in some way is the greatest satisfaction I've had throughout this whole endeavor.

About the Author

Morgan Boecher has been making comics ever since he was a youngster in Florida. His educational focuses were in anthropology, social work, and traveling the world. Now living in the New York City area, he uses his learning to market nonprofit music festivals and create art.